Deadlines

Jim Greenhalf

graft
poetry

CONTENTS

Roll Over, Philip Larkin

Some might see Jim Greenhalf simply as an "it's grim oop North" miserabilist, an aged Boomer sunk in nostalgia and narcissism or a sententious public polemicist. Unfortunately, in his stubborn, cross-grained way, he may have unwittingly invited these mis-readings, for he tends to shun the limelight. But not always.

Fortunately, there have been occasions in the past when his strengths have stirred due recognition. I vividly remember attending a poetry reading in the Bath House pub, Soho, on an April evening in 2005 when his singing of his religious poem 'Mary Magdalene' brought the young, metropolitan audience to its feet.

What are Greenhalf's strengths? I would highlight his honesty, humour and compassion, as well as his easy accessibility and his striking ability to fuse gravity with sensitivity. While some of his work is more declamatory in nature, much is astonishingly delicate:

At the going down of the sun.
An eye blinks.
A shivering drop of water pearls.
An orchid leaf reverberates

This latest collection displays all of his talents in their fullest, maturest bloom and especially his exacting ear and eye for precisely the right word and image. Its title

Deadlines is particularly apt, given his long career writing under the pressure as a journalist on all manner of subjects:

> Deadlines were my lifeline,
> I liked the pressure:
> compiling copy against the clock
> was the best education.

The title is also apt in that Greenhalf is struggling to come to terms with the pressure of another deadline – his own mortality – and, looking back, is striving to make sense of the conundrum of his own life and life in general. The word is further appropriate as a title, given Greenhalf's underlying sense that history and the very fabric of society is reaching some sort of ripping point.

The central poem which lends the collection its title takes us on an odyssey through his life and career, a journey studded with sharply humorous cameos of the politicians and celebrities he interviewed and the streets through which he roamed. He has no equal when it comes to capturing *zeitgeist* – the sights, sounds, sweats and smells of past decades, especially the Sixties. If the Boomer generation needs a memorialist, it should surely be Jim Greenhalf. The poem bears comparison with Ginsburg's 'Howl' in depicting a cultural moment – but without the breathlessness. He recalls how:

> The Age of Aquarius arrived at Paddington
> bearing posters of Che Guevara, Mao Tse Tung
> and Ho, Ho, Ho Chi Minh. Cuban heels, cheesecloth,

skinny-rib jumpers, bob cuts and military regalia …
… the slogans bloomed
like napalm's hot-house flowers …
I watched the sad sick spirit of the times
foaming like bicarbonate of soda in the veins …

About the Beatles terminal rooftop gig and Lennon's subsequent assassination, he writes:

Thursday afternoon, January 30, 1969

Something ended that cold afternoon.
None of us heard the sound of it ascending
off-the-cuff from the Savile Row roof of Apple.
Thirteen days after my twentieth birthday …

It only takes a breath, a turn of the screw
or the spin of a bullet, to make sure.
On Sunday, December 8, 1980, the shooter knew.
Hope remains up in the air.

But Greenhalf, deploying and focusing his artful blend of double vision, constantly juxtaposes past and present – a present that spans the tackily reinvented streets of Haworth in 'Keeper' or the big asks of today in 'One Word of Truth'.

He is not only engaging but deeply engaged and committed. In his reflections of and responses to social realities, he could be said to have pioneered a whole new literary genre: poetic journalism. In his poem 'Telling Sid' he picks up on that glib advertising slogan for the

Thatcherite privatisations of the 1980s, 'Tell Sid', fast-forwarding it to the 2020s and tracing how, like the hectic Sixties and hung-over Seventies before it, the greedy materialism and hollow aspirations of that decade have long since dissipated:

> We saw the Sixties wiped out;
> the Seventies bundled up in refuse bags;
> but the Eighties were good for you …
> buying up houses and shares
> when the country was being flogged.
> Now it's flooded with debt,
> cradle to grave; and you are older,
> dyspeptic and blue …
>
>   Look at you now:
> a three-car hacienda
> embedded among green acres,
> new-build for strangers,
> fearful of foreigners. And more:
> governments fit only for the wrecking ball,

As a man Greenhalf is northern to his core but, having been born and brought up in the South, he can bring to bear the exquisitely sharp dual perspective of the émigré. For instance in 'Preferred Lies' he describes with subtle poignancy the dull existence of a retired couple of displaced expats, returned 'home' from a privileged life in Rhodesia and South Africa and now trapped between golf course and nail salon beneath the droning planes of Heathrow ('Our life has gone into this arrangement').

Abandoning his usual voice, he tells it through their own words in a masterpiece of mimetic ventriloquence.

Nor does Greenhalf stop at the shores of Britain. In earlier work he had vividly evoked sojourns in Prague, Berlin, Paris and Brussels. In *Deadlines* Europe's current crisis in the Ukraine is also referenced with lethal obliqueness in his poem 'Cloudburst in July':

> Sauron in his Kremlin tower
> watches Gondor burn
>
> while we wonder what matters,
> more or less
>
> during a cloudburst in July,
> and debate what's best
>
> to eat for dinner
> and who to watch
>
> before we say God bless,
> and close our eyes.

But all of his poems, however deeply rooted in past or present realities, twist back to his quest to make sense of his own identity and values. As he has written, 'the power of recollection is not archival, antiquarian: the past comes right into the present because it has been rolling along with me, as it does for all of us, if we are open to it'.

Greenhalf can verge on stridency at times but there is nothing simplistic about his stance. As he writes, he walks 'a wire across the page' and treads doubtfully, uncertainly:

> What is it, then –
> a trip, a jaunt, a journey,
> a pilgrimage, a lark?
> Alone or with companions,
> it's an act of faith,
> outcome unknown,
> a shot in the dark.
>
> Fact and fiction: art and life
> Where does one begin the other?
> Are we then mostly pretending to be
> someone other than who we are,
> or haven't yet discovered?'

Picking a path in these wokist times is, he admits, a daunting challenge:

> Ezra Pound declared: *Make it news!*
> But who can do that now that apologies are all the
> rage?

Like many a big man Greenhalf is riddled with doubts and insecurities – which he candidly confesses:

> Too shy, too conscious of bloody me,
> me, me. *Greenhalf.* How I hated my name,
> ridiculed at junior and secondary school

All the same, he finds the strength to look beyond himself and to gaze – with clouded hope – into the future:

> supporting us
> is the hope
> of a false ending,
> the chance to start again.

And, despite castigating the current generation at one point, he is proud to admit that:

> I like hearing the stories of those
> younger than me, lucky or angry;
> risking responsibilities in unfamiliar places;
> not blaming or badging others.
> Thank God they're not like me.
>
> Why would I want them to be?
> I'm neither a template nor a fashion-plate …
> Don't camp among my foothills,
> go beyond the *roots that clutch and cling*
>
> Rise and fall and then, unlike us,
> surprise yourself again.

Greenhalf has his faults. In his earlier work he often wrote too much and too long and sometimes found it hard to lift his foot off the editorialising loud pedal. He also tended to overload his poems with obscure literary or personal references. Nevertheless, even in these poems if you hack your way through his thicket of allusions, you will find yourself a wonderfully bright, if bleak, upland – a Northern moorland, if you like – whose sweeping views carry you to new and surprising horizons

With the publication of *Deadlines,* Greenhalf now sits atop a heavy volume of past work – some fourteen published books and pamphlets. Those interested in his literary trajectory – and it demands interest – might usefully turn to earlier collections like *The Dog's Not Laughing: Poems 1966 – 1998* or especially *Cromwell's Head* (2023). *Deadlines* represents a further pinnacle, though not, one hopes, a farewell. He has long been accorded recognition among small presses, little magazines and poetry readings but now is the time for him to be celebrated even more widely and justly.

In one poem Greenhalf prays for the tenacity to go on developing artistically:

> Do not let me slip
> or lose my grip.
> You haven't seen
> my real size yet.

There you have it: both a prayer and a promise for the future. So go out and buy this book and read it again and again. And if fair judgement follows, then roll over Philip Larkin and tell Simon Armitage the news!

Peter Snow

And so hold on to the best things
    of the awakened mind.
Only the most solid and intangible
    aspects of the human spirit
can save us from succumbing
    to the waves of panic
that engulf us temporarily.

Ben Okri, from 'Mental Fight: An Anti-Spell for the 21st Century'

Pictures

Was this the shape that wet the lips of a thousand chicks
and hiked the ragged heights of Striding Edge?
Forgive the exaggeration, but whoa!
Is that rumpled, grumpy-looking tub of lard really me?
No wonder those old blue trousers won't go on.
How did my Promethean features sag and bloat so
                                     quickly?
Mirror, mirror on the wall: if you were a painting,
you'd fall and the glass would crack.
What's the point of jogging on the spot like a demonic
                                    Irish dancer
on a road-drill, or jerking those bar-bells up and down?
Where is the me I didn't mind looking at?
What's gone wrong?

Other abstainers much older than I am
don't look like I do.
Is it the side-effects of the necessary pills I take,
family, senescence, the century
or too much ale and cake?
I should be flayed, stuffed and put up as a dirigible on
                                    public display.
As for the fucker I used to be,
I've lost sight of him
over the hemisphere of this Sumo belly.

April 2023

15

Keeper

Thursday, a cold June morning,
exiled on Main Street, Haworth.
Whiling away the waiting time
watching tattooed arms and legs,
trainers, toy dogs, unwilling children
slogging up the hill and down again.
The Villette bakery's opposite,
the full English an attraction.

What was it when the Brontës
scuffed their clogs on the flinting setts,
before John Brown
laid most of them to rest?
St Michael's and all Angels
did not have tall trees then,
nor the soundtrack of jackdaws
cawing Naw! Naw! Naw!

The Wave of Nostalgia bookshop
declares itself the home of strong women.
I am still looking for one of them.
Ladies, in my experience,
strong women have nothing to prove.
I should know. I am the dog called Keeper.
Where would Emily go without me?

Cloudburst in July

Sauron in his Kremlin tower
watches Gondor burn,

while we wonder what matters,
more or less,

during a cloudburst in July,
and debate what's best

to eat for dinner
and who to watch

before we say God bless,
and close our eyes.

Get Back
Thursday afternoon, January 30, 1969

Something ended that cold afternoon.
None of us heard the sound of it ascending
off-the-cuff from the Savile Row roof of Apple.
Thirteen days after my twentieth birthday.

Some say the Sixties ended with the Tet Offensive,
the killings at Kent State, another dead Kennedy,
Belfast, Londonderry. If the age still had a soundtrack
of hope, optimism, in spite of bombs and gunshots,

it ended when plugs were pulled on a makeshift stage.
Goodbye George, Ringo, Paul and John,
goodbye and thank you Billy Preston.
Where was I? Was I even in the college annexe,

FE habitat of barefoot Sally, fainting at Holocaust
                                              newsreels;
Angela, face peering out of a black sunflower corona
of corkscrew hair, her barbed-wire handwriting,
and passion for Nazi history, American football and
                                              poetry?

Iain Sinclair might have been showing Stan Brakage,
Jonas Mekas films in Liberal Studies,
or mulling over the Allen Ginsberg shoot when
nervy Dutch cameraman Robert left the lens-cap on.

Perhaps Georgie Fame was waking after a night
at Ronnie Scott's. Five storeys above where he was,
PC Ray Dagg, chin-strap biting his lower-lip,
put his shoulder to the law's wheel and enforced it.

London's first free rooftop concert stopped.
He was thirteen when Please, Please Me broke the ice
of that long freezing winter of 1963, when the cold
was killing and Sylvia Plath turned up the gas.

It only takes a breath, a turn of the screw
or the spin of a bullet, to make sure.
On Sunday, December 8, 1980, the shooter knew.
Hope remains up in the air.

Changing Trains, Changing Times

Too young to notice the Fifties leaving the station –
Pat Boone, Alma Cogan and Frankie Vaughan
looking backwards as the diesel took them
away from girls screaming at hirsute musicians.

The Age of Aquarius arrived at Paddington
bearing posters of Che Guevara, Mao Tse Tung
and Ho, Ho, Ho Chi Minh. Cuban heels, cheesecloth,
skinny-rib jumpers, bob cuts and military regalia

from the rajah days of Empire were already in.
Some made a great leap forward, others took a trip
Up the Junction or Round the Horne.
Skirts went up and knickers went Down Your Way

with Franklein Engelman. Records were LPs,
not yet albums. Long before they hit the moon
Americans were shooting up Kennedys and Kings,
the jungles of Vietnam.

The Sixties departed in clouds of saffron dust
as hairless dancers chanted Hare Krishna,
and news presenters talked of Agent Orange,
napalm and collateral damage.

The Seventies brought in 'The Ascent of Man'
insurgencies, denim and Black September.
The currency changed.
All Our Yesterdays piled like bin-bags.

Somewhere between Baker's Alms
and Albion Square I lost myself.

The Roses of Sarajevo

Apparition Hill, in the town of Medjugorje, Bosnia, is where the Mother of Christ appeals for prayer and penitence.

In the capital city of Bosnia
two hundred scars at taxi-ranks, bus stops,
market places, on buildings,
mark the spot where people were murdered
by Serbian mortar-bombs,
fired from surrounding hills.
Painted or splattered red:
these are the Roses of Sarajevo.

It all starts innocently enough –
the questing mind,
the trusting heart,
the longing to escape
from where you are
to where you want to be,
if you know.

I didn't.
I was just afraid to go.
What is sought is rarely found –
I did not know –
in places that maps assign.

And I am like the river:
andante, allegretto, allegro –

always too fast or too slow
on the uptake. And the way
always rocky.

What is it, then –
a trip, a jaunt, a journey,
a pilgrimage, a lark?
Alone or with companions,
it's an act of faith,
outcome unknown,
a shot in the dark.

Where I am is what I know –
fifteen hundred miles or more
from Apparition Hill
where people pray or grieve.

Ash, ash,
is all the ash
the Roses of Sarajevo
leave.

Prayers

Fearfully, the tribes
entrusted their bullion
and, in the absence
of God and Moses,
returned to pagan rites –
the fire and light of visibility;
and, knowing the constant
worth of livestock,
put their faith in a cow.

Heavens, there are too many
madonnas already:
worshipped, polished,
idolised.

I am forever saying:
O bring me or take me
where you are near.

Do not drop out
of the bottom of my life.
Do not let me slip
or lose my grip.
You haven't seen
my real size yet.

Flags

Sticks and drones will break my bones;
but names make news editors
and television continuity announcers
issue warnings.

Rockets shoot up and bombs rain down,
whetting the edge of the knife.
Flag-wavers punch the air and jab their fists.
Everywhere the quality of mercy drains.

If there must be flags, let them be stones
that bridges, viaducts and grand canals have known,
not the stained and shredded rags
of a promised land.

Manacles Minus Houdini

It's like a jungle sometimes/ It makes me wonder
How I keep from goin' under – Grandmaster Flash and
the Furious Five

No, I don't remember where I was
when Enoch Powell made that speech,
the year after the Summer of Love
when Haight-Ashbury asphodels were rotting;
and love beads dropped off the balcony
of the Lorraine Motel;
and all the dogs of war were frothing.

But I do remember the slogans bloomed
like napalm's hot-house flowers:
White Power, Black Power;
integration, segregation, repatriation;
democracy is hypocrisy.

I watched the sad sick spirit of the times
foaming like bicarbonate of soda in the veins,
and in the tributaries of London.
East London Afro-Caribbean kids
suddenly looked sullenly at me,
if they looked at me at all.

And where was whitey?
They said: *stuck on the Moon.*
Dope on a rope with his nose in a spoon.
Close to the edge, half-expecting

machete-wielding attacks
on every bill-boarded corner,
enslaved by Enoch's hammering idea
of the black man having the 'whip-hand'.

I hear the voice of Marley's ghost –
Rise up, rise up –
but mind-forged manacles
everywhere, fear's old jungle-jangle.
And no holy Houdini anywhere
to unlock or untangle.

One Word of Truth

In response to your latest request for aid –
a bank transfer to buy baby milk–
please understand: I am not a general store,
a branch of your High Street bank,
nor the local arm of International Rescue.
I understand you have issues, addictions,
to add to your problems of making ends meet;
but do you? Save up, cut down, or here's an idea,
change the habits that you cannot afford.
Acquire others: clear up the dog shit
in your back yard; take in your washing
when it rains; smoke your dope in another place.
You've not been evicted, invaded or forced
by Holocaust, Holodomor or Nakba
to leave the country in a rubber-bottomed boat;
nor do the black cars of money-lenders
slide outside your house at night.
Your life still belongs to you. Next time
you feel compelled to knock,
just for a change, ask us if we're doing all right.

Deadlines

I

Fact and fiction: art and life.
Where does one begin the other?
Why does the fact that I was in London, 1965,
when Winston Churchill and T S Eliot died,
seem a meaningful coincidence?

Because my mind likes finding patterns
linking disparate experiences.
It also likes drop-intros and juxtaposition:
at the height of the Summer of Love –
August, 1967 – Kenneth Halliwell,

before killing himself, cratered like an egg
the crown of Joe Orton's head.
Foreboding and a sinking feeling
sent me wandering, Liverpool Street,
Blackfriars, sometimes the wild West End,

breathing the air of paper and print.
The dark glass of Fleet Street,
the Express's tinted 'Black Lubyanka'
where Chapman Pincher wrote about Blake,
Burgess, Philby and Maclean.

I could not see myself in there.
My old grey-haired overcoat,
worn like a habit winter and summer,
I passed immaculately-suited Sammy Davies Junior,
brow furrowed, walking in Mayfair.

House-lights down in the Aldwych Theatre,
Ben Hur sat in front of me
for Peter Brook's 'A Midsummer Night's Dream'.
I did not say hello. I saw Jennie Lee,
Aneurin Bevan's widow,

and W H Auden in carpet slippers
reciting 'The Shield of Achilles'.
Most of the others read from the page.
Even then I knew – though I wanted to be
a footballer not a hack.

The sight of Bob Light's new
green-grey portable Olivetti typewriter
(earned by a summer job painting tower block
window frames) changed all that.
Football was dropped for poetry, girls and books.

II

I always knew I was a bloody journalist!
Observing, recording, compiling lists –
football teams, Indian tribes, Bonaparte's battles.
I even wrote match reports for school assembly,
after another *the team played well* defeat.

Fact and fiction. Money, marriage, career?
Nothing is written, said Lawrence of Arabia.
After two years at Bradford College,
getting on at twenty-eight, I was offered
a writing job. I told Arnold Hadwin,

editor of the city's hot metal Telegraph
& Argus evening newspaper
that, great as his expectations might be,
I might not live up to them.
He said: *I think you can leave that to me.*

Ten years on miscellaneous news, politics,
learning to accept assignments,
bruising edits and deadening headlines;
then I was despatched South
to fill broadsheet pages with interviews.

The first was Denis Healey:
Anzio beach-master, Labour's deputy.
A bastard but not a shit – his own admission.
The Commons roared when he said
that reproof by Geoffrey Howe

was akin to being *savaged by a dead sheep.*
His Parthian shot at me –
Don't accept any wooden nickels –
suggested he was more amused than flattered
to be interviewed. Kingsley Amis was

another old devil who, like Healey,
fought in the war and didn't like what he saw
slouching towards Westminster.
(Those who give out prizes
gave him the Booker as a consolation).

He poured double measures of vodka
against winter's wind and rain,
and a miserable morning watching
Michael Heseltine back-comb his hair
into a perfect Simon Hoggart cliff.

Two or three days at a time
I'd be *In Town Tonight!* to fill my notebooks.
No expense account or hotels.
Amis, perhaps, took pity – especially
after realising I'd read his books,

some of them, sympathetically.
Once, out of Lancaster Gate tube,
I followed a downcast-looking worrier,
bags in one hand, briefcase in the other.
In FA headquarters, Bobby Robson

chaired his blue commuter's coat
in an office the size of a six-yard box.
A miner's son, who'd scored in England's
9-3 victory against the Scots,
now confined by different lines

he could not cross; but he gave me time.
Spoke of modern football yobs,
collar and tie men, not the feckless or hopeless
without proper jobs. All that was slovenly,
self-indulgent, arrogant, hacked

at his natural seam of decency.
When I asked Derek Jacobi
if gay Alan Turing in Hugh Whitmore's
'Breaking the Code', was really him, he said:
I like to try to be somebody or something I am not.

I always gave those who agreed to be
interviewed the chance to redact or rephrase:
I didn't consider myself a test they had to pass.
One word of truth can change the world,
Solzhenitsyn said in his Nobel speech.

Dispatched to Ravenscliffe estate
to door-step the parents of murdered
Bradford girl Carole Wilkinson,
I knocked and said: *Tell me to fuck off.*
Come in, lad, her dad replied instead.

III

Did I crassly say, *Mr Livingstone,*
I presume, when I met 'Red' Ken?
At the time, Labour was divorcing itself
from reality – Roy Jenkins the plaintiff,
Tony Benn, the accused.

Livingstone survived Mrs Thatcher's
torpedoing of the GLC, bobbing up
like Ishmael, on a back-bench.
He saw her being stabbed in the back
while he smiled on. It was his humour

to smile when he went on the attack.
The charm of a lounge-lizard
matched a passion for botany and politics.
Power's said to be an aphrodisiac.
He didn't seem fazed or aroused by it;

but, I have to admit,
in buxom Betty Boothroyd's
Speaker's office, I had the urge
to unbutton her blouse.
Party critics later said he was anti-semitic

for challenging Israel's Knesset.
The Board of Deputies of British Jews
hammered the final nail in.
Used to be Clause Four that separated
the righteous from the Gadarene Swine.

Norman Willis, General Secretary of the TUC,
shyly confessed to a strong weakness
for writing poetry. *Show me*, I said.
He did. I was impressed. In Congress House,
he read: 'Thoughts Upon a Comradely Address'.

I included it with the interview,
glad he got his wish to see his poetry
in print. I liked him for admitting
this humble ambition.
You can read it here at the back.

The Lady in Pink – Dame Barbara Cartland –
offered tea, cucumber sandwiches
and radical feminism of bygone days.
She held forth about the Thirties,
poverty and birth-control,

and why her seven hundred romances,
produced the way Ford assembled vehicles,
ran on high octane fidelity and sex
after marriage only.
Had she never succumbed to temptation,

a flash-fire of need she could not resist?
I didn't ask. Why tell an evening
provincial newspaper when she could sell
the world a love story spicier
than the ones that flew off her wrist?

She insisted on word-proofing my article.
Dictating to a secretary was more her style,
not scribbling shorthand hieroglyphics,
checking names, dates, spellings.
Time was her luxury. I didn't have it.

IV

Deadlines were my lifeline,
I liked the pressure:
compiling copy against the clock
was the best education.
The best can do it unscripted.

I watched Gay Byrne one Friday morning,
at the Donnybrook studios of RTE;
sleeves rolled, listening and arguing
with callers on his radio phone-in –
God, Catriona of Portmarnock

is not going to like this!
After lunch, a nap, he was back
for The Late Late Show cameras –
two hours, sometimes three, open-ended
entertainment, argument, controversy:

the holy trinity lighting up the night
above the Republic. I didn't have
his gift of the gab and could be
apprehensive about opening my gob
in the presence of nobs, snobs and notables –

Lord Hailsham said my long hair was reprehensible.
My journalism tutor said I had yet to learn
the importance of dress to a news-gatherer.
Never ask the first question; leave conferences last;
don't follow the pack. That's what I learned.

I once watched Alex Ferguson
conquer a roomful of St James Park hacks –
leather-coats, boozy faces –
simply by smiling nicely at all of them.
Talking to people: the job I least liked doing.

Too shy, too conscious of bloody me,
me, me. *Greenhalf.* How I hated my name,
ridiculed at junior and secondary school.
My mother almost made things worse
by naming me Graham. Imagine.

Hello Mr Amis, I'm Graham Greenhalf.
Marginally worse than Alan Bennett
having a Gordon for kin.
I wasn't Ian McKellen or Derek Jacobi –
perfectly themselves as someone else.

If all the world really is *a stage*,
as literature's greatest hack has Jacques say,
are we then mostly pretending to be
someone other than who we are,
or haven't yet discovered?

Took me nigh on half a century –
eighteen to sixty-eight –
travelling, remembering, collating,
writing bloody endlessly.
Nowadays does anyone even leave the office?

V

Hunting celebrities was a Red-top blood-sport.
The Sun had to pay Elton John a million,
damages for allegations that did not stand up
in court. Phone-hacking, that later put paid
to The News of the World, was still off-page.

I would not have done it anyway.
I once pissed off an editor by refusing
to write MPs a round-robin letter
on the *vital importance* of an unfettered press.
There should be controls, I told him.

I'd heard the tales in the pub,
abuse and intrusion where there was
no public interest, even stealing
family mementoes after a 'tragic death'.
C P Scott's *Comment is free but facts are sacred*

evidently meant nothing to some.
It meant nothing to me until my first by-lined
piece on death and the Brontës.
My hated name didn't matter so much,
once associated with something

other than me. I asked Alan Bennett
if he thought writers were shits.
Chekhov, Kafka he said, *weren't like that.*
Poets were *alcoholics, manic-depressives*
or were likely to be.

Philip Larkin was all right, I suppose,
but he wasn't a load of laughs.
I had to go back to Finchley Road
to meet the melancholy Rabbi Lionel Blue:
Harry Worth with anxiety,

a code-breaker too on the QT –
then. A communal bowl of food
for all to share was his ideal;
but really he wanted an argument
with Yahweh, about the Holocaust

and all the wickedness triumphing daily.
Apart from a few 'Thought for the Day'
minutes on the BBC and a bit of telly,
all he had was the promise
of a page by me.

After it was finished,
he asked me to stay and taste
a bowl of borscht.
After a morning of death and God,
the dish was a penance I could not stomach.

Few of the rich and famous I interviewed
had GCE'A' Levels or a degree.
Self-belief made the difference.
Their lives affirmed what I always I knew.
That's the truth I tried to communicate.

Journalism's supposed to comfort the afflicted
and afflict the comfortable; entertain,
enlighten and illuminate.
Tony Harrison tried to make poetry do that
in newspapers and on television.

'The Gaze of the Gorgon', 'The Cycles of Donji Vakuf',
made him a poet-reporter in Bosnia,
and at his parents' grave in Leeds.
He knew the value of poetry on the front page –
away from arts, crafts and book reviews.

Ezra Pound declared: *Make it news!*
But who can do that now that apologies are all the rage?
Jean Rook goodbye. All words eventually fade.
Yes, yes, mortality, we know;
but don't let facts rattle your cage.

VI

Old Philip, deliverer of mail and newspapers,
a guardian of time at the T&A,
used to warn us: *Be careful – otherwise*
you might end up as a paragraph.
I'm still waiting for mine.

July to December, 2023

False Endings

When have the times
not threatened Armageddon?
The bullet that passed
through the heart

of the last century
still rifles through this one.
When all the storms
whirling out of the sky

have ripped the earth
like a lid from a tin;
when all the lies
have exiled the truth

and closed the borders
to faith and reason;
when dust and ashes
thickly drift and the time

we have to risk the gift
we failed to bless
flat-lines on a screen;
the only pillar left

supporting us
is the hope
of a false ending,
the chance to start again.

Lucky John

*Lord Lucan's Victorian ancestor the Third Earl of Lucan
led the notorious Charge of the Light Brigade during the
Anglo-French war against Russia in 1854.*

Just as fat men get nicknamed 'slim',
they called John Bingham,
Seventh Earl of Lucan,
'Lucky'.

Merchant banker, Mayfair gambler,
the gallants urged him on,
ever deeper into the valley of debt.
It was a killing.

After all, what's the loss
of a few hundred
or even a few thousand?
He thought himself among the gods.

They smiled at him
as he charged onwards,
between chance and folly
and changing odds.

Though he lost the money
that others earned,
he thought he was fire-proof –
until he got burned.

Renaissance Man

I was waiting for him
below a hilltop cemetery.
A roar of laughter
from the back seat
of a yellow taxi:

Ha! You're here!
Spirit on the water,
spirit in the air.
I'd flown in from
the benighted isles,

hoping for readings,
excitement, flare.
And suddenly,
there he was.
And here we were,

eight hundred miles
from the Acropolis,
Bradford,
where his big idea –
poetry cabaret

in Prague –
arose like a sprite
in the mid-morning
steam of
Americanos.

His smile,
like the slow
removal of a £50 note
from a black wallet,
said anything was possible.

He conjured up
a welcoming feast –
red wine, white wine,
lamb, chicken, beef
piled on silver platters.

He kept disappearing,
like Harry Lime;
more food, more drink,
kept arriving.
All on tick.

His fridge, like his life,
jammed with pâtê,
cheeses, salami,
delicatessen delicacies
past their sell-by date.

Live now – pray later.
He said: *Drive*
without rear-view mirrors.
Only thing that matters
is the way ahead.

Fast Davie:
behind his back,
creditors, bankruptcies,
receipts, discarded
in a drawer.

I found screw-top jars
crammed with
uncounted coins:
three or four thousand
in ready cash.

And further back
than my organising
mind could reach:
a wife, his third,
a son, a house.

I got my shows –
The Globe,
with Vladimir Merta,
cafés in Mala Strana
with Alice Bauer

and Jaroslav Hutka,
Charles University
where students,
impatient to know
the route to wealth's

yellow brick road,
were bored by me.
I flew out nine
hundred pounds
lighter; but ruefully

richer, thanks to
a rogue Prospero,
who vanished
like my money.
No problemo!

Sometimes, it seems,
the world needs rogues
to drive our dreams.

Preferred Lies

*In golf, during bad weather a ball may be moved to a
different 'lie'*

We've got Bombay Sapphire,
or good old B&S
if you prefer?

Bit of a shock
after Salisbury, East London,
but not a bad spot –

planes taking off
over Runnymede, sun
going down over Reading,

the view of the A30!
We did think about Beckenham,
but Joan's from Camberley

and Vicky lives with Gavin
in Lightwater. We don't go there much.
You have to take your shoes off.

I told them: if this is a place of worship,
put a mat down facing east
and I'll say a prayer.

They're particular. For their anniversary
Gavin made tapas, Vicky made sangria.
We left early. She had a hangover,

Saturday to the Monday.
I know. That's what we told her.
She said: 'I'm on the sick.

They can't get rid of me!' Anyway,
here we are. The balcony overlooks
Prince Edward and Sophie's estate –

behind the wire, that pale fencing.
Don't suppose we'll bump into them
at M&S. Shame about Queenie.

Her Golden Jubilee it was, when we left.
Village had a butcher's then,
car show-room. Now it's all nail bars

and hair salons. Jack's Famous
Fish and Chip Shop's gone.
All retirement flats like this one.

Lot of Blacks from Africa
now. For the homes
mostly. Bit like Harare.

Thanks for risking your tyres,
driving over. The road's
a shocker. Yes. Like the country.

Still, the club's only
a tee or two away.
And as Johnny says,

you can see the Surrey hills
on a good day.
Ascot's one stop down the track,

Windsor's a stone's throw.
So is Heathrow.
Some evenings we'll sit here,

looking up, wondering
how high they're flying.
Where they're going.

Our life's gone into this arrangement.
You can get used to anything –
that's what Gavin says.

Doll's House

Red-brick: an Edwardian vicarage,
sixty-foot trees towering over it.
A life-size brick doll's house
in the back garden,
the welded steel skeleton
of an ocean-going sailing-boat,
outside the red front door,
hinted at eccentricities
within.

A glass cabinet the size
of the windowed café
in Edward Hopper's 'Nighthawks',
crammed with doll babies,
dozens, scores perhaps.
Glassy-eyed porcelain buddhas,
silent, watchful, waiting

for Dr Frankenstein,
a flash of lightning,
to climb out
of that sarcophagus;
crawl over rugs,
unbolt the front door
and, under owl-night,

start goose-stepping,
towards me;
arms reaching,

eyes fixed
like bayonets.

Aborted ideals,
unrequited loves,
dead sisters and mothers,
sons and daughters
I do not have.

Borrowed Time

Remembering Maggie Silver, Bridget Baker and Lisa Singleton

Gone. Finally. Out of reach.
March to September.
The other side of sleep.

Morning wood pigeons'
bravo, bravo
will not wake them
today, tomorrow,
my dark ladies.

Just another passing through,
like traffic on the A322.

Orchids in the sink.
Blinds shuttered.
The crump of guns.
That hopeful subaltern,
still motoring along the old A30,
with Joan Hunter-Dunn.

At the going down of the sun.
An eye blinks.
A shivering drop of water pearls.
An orchid leaf reverberates.

One by one
they disappear:
under the hill, up in the air:
all our sad captains,
all our dead dears.

After Tollund Man

They won't have to go as far as Aahrus
to exacavate me.
Should some probing literary palaeontologist,
stub his toe on my body
of work,

they'll just have to weigh up
how much will be worth their while
to air-brush back into history.
How did this get here? they'll say,
trying to identify – belatedly –

an old fossil's place in their scheme of things.
A relic of the age of typewriters,
small presses, libraries.
There are too many already, they'll say,
in charity shops, on ebay;

unlike Danish 'Tollund Man'.
I, of course, will be no bloody use to them,
buried under so many layers.
We'll need another Heaney, they'll say,
to dig this bollock-walloper up again.

Telling 'Sid'

*'Sid' was a fictional Everyman in a Conservative
Government advertising campaign in the early 1980s for
selling shares in national utilities to create a 'share-
owning democracy'.*

Lewis serves me coffee
in the New Albion.
He wants to join the Royal Marines
to scupper piracy on the high seas,
people trafficking, drug-smuggling.

Half-a-century younger than I am,
he lives the sense old lubbers like us ignore:
the triumph of hope over experience.
Travel, he believes, does more
than broaden the mind;

it intensifies empathy's tidal-pull,
like work, makes individuals
entrenched in habit and isolation
less likely to be hostage
to anger, fear, anxiety.

You used to believe that too,
Travelling ad hoc across continents,
following Afghani Gold and Patchouli
girls, jingle-jangling their bangles
overland to Katmandu,

bead-bags full of Siddhartha,
Motorcycle Maintenance,
and Kahlil Gibran;
no mobies or silicon devices
then. Look at you now:

a three-car hacienda
embedded among green acres,
new-build for strangers,
fearful of foreigners. And more:
governments fit only for the wrecking ball

that give way too easily
to those hell-bent on subterfuge,
revision or defeat; the young ripped off,
disaffected, dismayed,
falling for any crackpot idea,

agitating against authority;
this *other Eden*, burrowed by rats;
as for the elderly, you and me,
we're finished: we're done, done, done.
How many times since atomic bombs

and hydrogen bombs
have I heard myself recite a similar litany?
And how many times have ordinary acts
or extraordinary art
rolled me back from Barry McGuire's

'Eve of Destruction',
Shangri-la or Armageddon:
we damn or save ourselves.
The sad, sick world's lost its footprints
in the dust of 9/11.

Nothing travels faster
than the light of a dying star –
except bad news. Nothing unravels
the threads of reason faster
than armchair generals and Jeremiahs.

But the world's heard it all before:
Matthew Arnold, stranded on Dover Beach;
Oswald Spengler, declining in the West;
and Hugh Selwyn-Mauberley,
Ezra Pound's defeated poet,

roaring at a post-war *botched civilisation,*
an old bitch, gone in the teeth.
But the dog's still twitching.
For those shackled to a thought,
a clause or apocalyptic prophecy:

the world you wait to ambush you
has rolled this way
one hundred and sixty times or more,
since the Romans left Britain
and Extinction Rebellion –

the Great Rapture:
the Great Tribulation:
the Last Judgement.
The future was nailed up long ago
outside the walls of Jerusalem.

I used to feel like that, estranged,
threatened; to a degree I still do.
We saw the Sixties wiped out;
the Seventies bundled up in refuse bags;
but the Eighties were good for you:

buying up houses and shares
when the country was being flogged.
Now it's flooded with debt,
cradle to grave; and you are older,
dyspeptic and blue.

Times are turbulent and old men,
as they always do, invest in doom.
I am, on bad days, just like you,
unless a song, a scene, a kindness,
the memory *of a lovely fuck*,

re-connects past and present including,
yes, a few crackpot idealists: Peggy Duff,
Gunther Wallraff, Betty Williams –
all, without murdering martyrdom,
agitators against authority.

In his last dying days old acid A A Gill
wrote about the impossibility
of being racist with a terminal disease
in NHS hospitals.
One man loved is bound to be

a problem for another man
who feels unloved, passed over,
dissed. More than one climate
nourishes the planet. And so I listen
as Lewis serves me coffee.

I like hearing the stories of those
younger than me, lucky or angry;
risking responsibilities in unfamiliar places;
not blaming or badging others.
Thank God they're not like me.

Why would I want them to be?
I'm neither a template nor a fashion-plate,
to the Ben Stokes generation.
Don't camp among my foothills,
go beyond the *roots that clutch and cling*.

Rise and fall and then, unlike us,
surprise yourself again.

November 2023 – February 2024

Illusionists

No one really knows
what happened to Flight MH370,
Kuala Lumpa to Beijing,
that early March morning, 2014.
If a Boeing 777 can disappear
with 239 people, without warning,
well…

The bleeders who lead us
know how to eliminate
hundreds, thousands, millions,
whole countries even…
Map-makers alone did not
reduce Poland to a rumour,
twice. Sometimes I think
we're a bad idea in the mind of God.

Come on, Faustus,
by sleight of hand transform
everything mad or bad
or, for a leaf-falling moment,
make me think it has all disappeared.
Suspend my disbelief –
like the wire between Twin Towers
walked by Philip Petite,
that windy New York morning.

And when my transponders
no longer signal
an image in your eye,
I'll still be here,
walking a wire across the page.

Frost in November

In memory of Alexei Navalny

A square of scrubby grass,
bordered narrowly on three sides;
crab apple, plum, tomatoes,
clematis and wisteria –

a small patch of England.
Across the top of it aircraft
rise and dip, thirty thousand feet
above me. On good days

I watch them go by without me.
On days of November frost,
I think of Voltaire and Pasternak,
under more pressure than a fire-hose,

confined to their gardens.
Digging, weeding and planting,
at Ferney and Peredelkino,
gave their minds respite

from the murdering times.

Old Gobbo

What! Are you still here?

Like a Battersea dog
hoping to be chosen,
or a desert
without an ocean,
I wait for you.

Like a people
chosen for slaughter,
or the nameless
under ground or water,
I wait for you.

Like a moonlit shore
without a stranger,
or a byre
without a saviour,
I wait for you.

Acknowledgements

This book owes much to Nicholas Bielby, painter, poet and editor of Graft Poetry; Peter Snow, a trenchant critic of my writing for nearly twenty-five years and Dr Michael Stewart, poet, playwright, novelist and shrewdly observing critic.

Poetry by Jim Greenhalf

Andy Croft's Smokestack Books
- Cromwell's Head (2023)
- Dummy! (2021)
- Breakfast at Wetherspoons (2018)

The late David Tipton's Redbeck Press
- The Man in the Mirror (2010)
- Grassington's Reflex (2007)
- Blue on Blue (2005)
- In the Hinterland (2003)
- The Unlikelihood of Intimacy in the Next Six Hours (2001)
- Following the Seine (2000)
- The Dog's Not Laughing: Poems 1966-1998 (1999)

Poetry Pamphlets
- Out of Passion with the Times (1994)
- Battles (1980)
- Winter (1978)
- Porkfat's Complaint and Other Poems (1972)

Notes

p. 18: Iain Sinclair is a poet, novelist and 'geo-psychological' biographer of East London..

p. 26: The Lorraine Motel, Memphis, Tennessee, was where Martin Luther King Junior was shot dead on 4 April, 1968. 'Whitey on the Moon', a song-poem by Gill Scott-Heron, was released in January, 1970.

p. 29-40: The Express building in Fleet Street was nick-named 'The Black Lubyanka', after the KGB prison in Moscow, because of its tinted windows. Chapman Pincher wrote front-page articles about spies. Joe Orton was a playwright – 'a suburban Oscar Wilde'. Kenneth Halliwell was his lover. Ben Hur was Charlton Heston. The player of epic film roles was also an accomplished stage actor. Peter Brook's production of A Midsummer Night's Dream – white shag carpeting on the stage, swings and trapezes above it – was internationally acclaimed, though Charles Marowitz, the American founder of London's subterranean Open Space theatre, thought the 1970s needed something leaner and meaner after Brecht, Beckett and Osborne. Jean Rook was a Daily Express columnist who once likened John Wayne's hands to *big, brown saddlebags*.

p. 42: Anyone who hears a strain of Amy Winehouse's great song 'Love is a Losing Game' in part of the Lord Lucan poem is quite right.

p. 45: Singer-songwriters Vladimir Merta and Jaroslav Hutka were part of former Czechoslovakia's 'Velvet Revolution' in 1989 against the occupying Soviet empire. We did shows in Prague in 2007 along with Jazz/blues singer Alice Bauer.

p. 55-59: Peggy Duff, a founder of War Resisters International, was also a CND campaigner. A girlfriend told me about her. Bob Woodward and Carl Bernstein of the Washington Post, were inspirational for trainee journalists for their Watergate stories as portrayed by Robert Redford and Dustin Hoffmann in the 1976 film 'All the President's Men'. But Gunther Wallraff, a West German under-cover investigative reporter whose exploits I read about, probably took greater risks to get at the truth. Betty Williams shared the 1976 Nobel Prize for Peace with Mairead Corrigan for organising non-sectarian community peace groups in Belfast. We met at Bradford University in 2011 where she publicly condemned male Muslim 'honour killings' of young women. Ben Stokes, one of England's greatest all-round cricketers and captain of the exciting national cricket team whose playing philosophy is, 'commitment to the process but emotional detachment from the result'.

p. 62: Alexei Navalny, jailed by the Putin regime in Russia for speaking out against tyranny, was killed in captivity in February, 2024.

Sir John Betjeman (who confessed to Michael Parkinson that he thought he was no good as a poet), Alfred Lord Tennyson, Thom Gunn, Sylvia Plath, T S Eliot and John Berryman are among the poets whose work is referenced on pages 24, 43, 53, 54 and 59.

p. 67: The poem by the late Norman Willis, General Secretary of the Trades Union Congress (1984-1993), which he read when I interviewed him in 1988, is included below. I liked it then. I still do.

Thoughts upon a Comradely Address

'Comrade, that was a MIGHTY speech
It raised a MIGHTY cheer
As you savaged old White
Who FOUGHT for the right
For you to make it here.

Comrade, that was a TELLING speech
I could see by the look on your face
As you made them reject
A man I respect
Who honours a seat in this place.

Comrade, that was a MAGNIFICENT speech
Your words were a savage tool
But as I despised it
I recognised it
The words of an arrogant fool.

Comrade, that was an HISTORIC speech
But really not quite the worst
For, with venom and spleen
When I was eighteen
You see, I made it FIRST.'

Norman Willis

That was how it was then. Everything that grew took a long time to grow; and everything that ended took a long time to be forgotten…

'The Radetzky March', Joseph Roth, translation by Michael Hofmann